Butterflies Afield
in the PACIFIC NORTHWEST

Butterflies Afield

in the PACIFIC NORTHWEST

By William A. Neill

Photography by
Douglas J. Hepburn

Search
715 Harrison Street
Seattle, Washington 98109

For reviewing the manuscript or making suggestions,
we would like to thank the following:
Dr. Ernst J. Dornfeld, Professor of Zoology,
Oregon State University at Corvallis;
John Hinchliff, Portland;
Sanford Leffler, University of Washington, Seattle;
Dr. David V. McCorkle, Associate Professor of Biology,
Oregon College of Education at Monmouth;
Jonathan P. Pelham, Coordinator of the Northwest
Lepidoptera Survey, Seattle.

Cover and Book Design by Mal Weber

Cover Photo: Mating pair of silvery blues.
The female is on the left.

To Sara and Sissy,
Jim, Bill, and Valerie
(without their permission),
for the sunny roamings
in open places.

Contents

Seasons

For butterflies in the Pacific Northwest, spring begins in the eastern canyons of the Columbia Gorge, in those sheltered draws that are able to catch the sun. On the first clear days in late March, the early orange tip and spring azure are flying. New vegetation has just started on the branches stripped bare by winter. The sun's rays, still slanting from the south, are warm but tentative, not hot. The butterflies flit about in the patches of light or perch on rocks warmed by the sun. When the sun slides behind the low clouds lingering about the overhanging hills, the air is too cool, and the butterflies hide, for they depend upon the sun's radiant energy to stimulate their metabolism enough for flight.

It is almost two months later when the butterflies come out at Beaver Creek in the dry, open ponderosa woods of the Cascade Mountains' eastern slope. A broad, brilliant blue swath of sky cut through the treetops repeats the course of the creek below. The sun bears down hot and convincing. Hairstreaks, blues, coppers, whites, and swallowtails emerge together. Pausing in the sun on the red dirt path, they are wary and fly up as you approach, but on the wildflowers they seem preoccupied by the nectar and can be examined closely. In the afternoon, groups of butterflies sit along the creek with their drinking tubes uncoiled and thrust into the moist sand. In midsummer, this place will be parched. Dragonflies and lizards will still be there, but few butterflies.

By August, summer in the lowlands and prairie of the Northwest is old and dry; the butterflies are fewer, and some are worn and tattered. But the high mountain trails have been freed of snow for only a little while, and the primes of spring and summer have arrived there simultaneously. The fresh alpine meadows are filled with flowers and butterflies. You will see them if you go there.

Scaly Wings

Butterflies are animals and, more specifically, members of the class Insecta. As with all insects, they have three pairs of jointed legs and a tough, hard body covering which serves as an external skeleton. Butterflies and moths differ from other insects by having scaly wings, which is the basis of the name of their collective order, Lepidoptera. Although closely related, butterflies and moths can be distinguished from each other by several features. Butterflies are about only by day; moths, usually at night. Most often butterflies rest with their wings folded vertically over their backs; moths, with their wings held horizontally. Antennae of butterflies end in a knob; those of moths are pointed or feathered.

Metamorphosis

When it's winter high in the mountains, cold and white, no one sees the butterflies, though they are all around. These same slopes, now forbidding, were covered by butterflies last summer and will be again next summer. The butterflies are there in January, too, but in a form more suited to surviving the long, dark, icy winter. Pupae and minute but hardy eggs are attached securely to wind-tossed twigs. Others lie buried under the snow.

The scaly-winged adult, conspicuous and familiar to everyone, represents one of the four stages of development in the butterfly's life cycle. The other stages — egg, larva (or caterpillar), and pupa (or chrysalis) — are more retiring and accordingly, less widely known. This sequence of physical changes in the life cycle is called metamorphosis.

Eggs are cemented to the appropriate plant species by the fertilized adult female. A butterfly egg is one-twentieth of an inch or less in diameter, and in many species its tough shell is microscopically sculptured in the most intricate and beautiful detail.

The tiny infant larva, delicate and vulnerable as it emerges from the egg, fortunately has only a short distance to travel for its first meal. All growth of the butterfly occurs in the larval stage. The larva is an eating machine with just enough mobility to forage from leaf to leaf and not enough imagination to attract undesired attention from its many predators. Despite its voracious appetite, the larva is extremely fastidious about its diet. Some species accept only a single kind of plant and would perish before eating any substitute.

After completing its enormous growth with relatively little change in form, the larva abruptly becomes sedentary, attaches itself to the plant or drops to the ground, and within a day or two sheds its skin. The pupa that emerges remains physically inactive throughout its existence. Beneath its protective skin, however, occurs a dramatic transformation to the long-legged, winged, brightly painted, remarkable adult.

The legs and wings of the completed adult are compactly folded when it hatches from the pupa. The wings expand with the help of fluid forced into their supporting veins, and within an hour the butterfly can fly. Flight provides mobility, the mobility needed by the male in his quest for a mate and needed by the female in broadly dispersing her eggs. Dozens or hundreds of eggs may painstakingly be laid by a single successful female in order to balance the terrible losses to disease, parasites, and direct predation. Meanwhile, the male, having fulfilled his sole duty, lives a life of leisure among his flowers.

To continue its existence, a species of animal must maintain an unbroken thread of life through the most extreme adversities that it will encounter in its habitat. Each stage in a butterfly's life cycle possesses certain special capabilities as well as certain needs. The transition from one stage to the next must be carefully timed to correspond in the most advantageous way with the local seasonal changes. For example, the adults must be abroad together during sunny weather in order to mate and lay eggs, the larva must hatch when the vegetation of its food plant is fresh and tender, and a resilient stage capable of assuming a dormant attitude must be selected to face the winter. As a rule, most butterflies get through the Northwest winter as eggs or pupae, but each species develops its own strategy of matching the peculiarities of its life cycle and habitat.

Habitat

Adaptation of a species' life cycle to cope most successfully with one set of environmental conditions narrows its flexibility in dealing with different environments. Each butterfly successfully colonizes some habitats but not others. Specialization of the larva's diet is an obvious limiting factor; the butterfly certainly cannot propagate outside the geographic range of its food plant. We can assume that other less obvious but nonetheless important traits are disadvantageous for certain habitats, since a butterfly is by no means universally found even where its favorite food plant grows in abundance.

Human civilization has influenced butterfly ecology, usually in an adverse manner. Contamination of the environment with insecticides and other toxic chemicals has probably contributed to the documented decline in butterfly population in some regions of the United States. Probably more potent, however, is the effect of land use. An enormous amount of land has been converted from rough fields and open woods, which can support diverse butterfly species, into managed fields or forests where a narrow range of plants is cultivated. Moreover, even in uncultivated land in the Northwest, huge numbers of eggs, larvae, and pupae must be eaten or stepped on by cattle permitted to graze there. The construction of logging roads, on the other hand, seems to have extended slightly the range of some butterflies able to feed on the plants that grow along the opened roadsides.

It is possible to separate the Pacific Northwest into rather distinct geographic regions from the standpoint of butterfly ecology.
1   Olympic Mountains. The heavily forested, rugged mountains are topped by alpine meadows. Characteristic butterfly species: clodius parnassian (phoebus on the summits), acmon blue, and anise swallowtail.
2   Pacific coast to Cascade Mountains. This region consists mainly of low mountains and broad valleys. The intense cultivation of the flatlands and the rainy weather combine to keep the butterfly population low. Characteristic species: Sara's orange tip, silvery blue, and western tiger swallowtail.
3   West slope of Cascade Mountains. The forest is dense and wet, and the butterfly population low. Characteristic species: clodius parnassian, hydaspe fritillary, and Nevada arctic.
4   High Cascades. This alpine region is characterized by a severe winter, a short summer

growth period, and stunted plants. Milbert's tortoiseshell, mariposa copper, sooty hairstreak, and the many other butterflies among the wildflowers in high mountain meadows are a late summer delight for hikers.

5   East slope of Cascade Mountains. Only a few miles east of the crest the weather is drier, and the forest changes to an open, dry pine forest with manzanita and wildflowers neatly arranged beneath the trees. The variety and number of butterflies increase. Found here: western sulphur, snowberry checkerspot, and acmon blue.

6   High plateau of Columbia Basin. This is high semidesert extending over much of eastern Washington and Oregon and parts of Idaho and Nevada. Trees are scarce. Land that has not been converted to monotonous wheat fields is covered by sagebrush and scattered wildflowers. The resident butterflies prefer the canyons. Characteristic species: ochre ringlet, oetus wood nymph, and Behr's hairstreak.

7   Eastern Mountains. The Okanogan, Blue, Wallowa, Ochoco, and Steens mountains, although certainly not a single ecological unit, possess at least two features in common which influence their butterfly population: a relatively dry climate favorable for butterfly propagation and a link with the Rocky Mountains to the east. Field crescent, Butler's alpine, lustrous copper, and others widely distributed through the Rockies extend into these mountains, overlapping there with their West Coast relatives.

Species

Nearly 200 kinds of butterflies reside in the Pacific Northwest. The majority are easily recognizable since the individual members, although never identical, resemble one another enough to be distinguished clearly from members of other species. They are the products of ancestors that for a long time have bred only with one another, avoiding exchange of genes with other related species and thereby preserving a distinct gap in appearance from them. The absence of hybrids interposed between two closely related species does not always mean that they are incapable of cross-breeding. Cross-infertility is only one mechanism of species isolation and prevention of gene interchange. Separate species, which could produce viable hybrid offspring, may not interbreed because of varied circumstances, including geographic separation, different seasonal flight period, courtship ritual, or other behavioral patterns, which may be assumed to influence strongly their choice of mating partners.

Less commonly, the boundary between two species is blurred. When hybridization occurs, there may be great difficulty in assigning an individual butterfly to one species or the other, and controversy may even exist as to whether a separation of the total group into two species is scientifically valid. The official status of these species — for example, some of the fritillaries — is constantly changing, depending upon which specialists in nomenclature can mount the most convincing contemporary argument. A delight, of course, to enlightened scientists, this fluidity of life should prove disturbing only for those who insist upon the most tidy categorization of nature, according to human design. Nature is irregular and cannot be expected always to conform to rectangular specimen boxes, no matter how carefully labeled and prepared.

Each species is identified by a double scientific name written in boldface, for example, **Papilio rutulus.** The first name, capitalized, is the genus, a group of very closely related species. The second, not capitalized, refers to the individual species.

Although cumbersome to learn, the scientific names have the advantage of worldwide unambiguity (usually). Common names, such as "western tiger swallowtail," are easier. However, some species lack common names, and their use is somewhat inconsistent.

We assume that some readers will want to identify butterflies they encounter in the field by comparing what they see with the pictures in this book. With this objective in mind, we have categorized the species into groups that can be described by certain physical features, as in the following outline. This arrangement corresponds more or less to the scientific organization developed by lepidopterists.

Most Pacific Northwest species likely to be seen are pictured in this book. It has not been possible, however, to include every species. Some adventuresome readers, we hope, will range far enough afield to run into some of those we omitted, and will explore other books for more detailed information about butterflies.

Guide for Identification —
by color and other physical characteristics

Sulphurs, whites, and parnassians: bright yellow or
white with black markings

Colias occidentalis	Western sulphur
Pieris rapae	Cabbage white
Pieris napi	Veined white
Pieris occidentalis	Western white
Anthocaris sara	Sara's orange tip
Euchloe ausonides	Marble wing
Parnassius clodius	Clodius parnassian

Fritillaries, checkerspots, and crescents: orange with
black and silver spots

Speyeria callippe	Callippe fritillary
Speyeria hydaspe	Hydaspe fritillary
Speyeria zerene	Zerene fritillary
Speyeria mormonia	Mountain fritillary
Speyeria leto	Leto fritillary
Euphydryas colon	Snowberry checkerspot
Boloria selene	Silver-bordered fritillary
Boloria epithore	Western meadow fritillary
Phyciodes campestris	Field crescent
Phyciodes mylitta	Mylitta crescent

Anglewings: ragged wing margins; underside dead
leaf pattern

Polygonia satyrus	Satyr anglewing
Polygonia zephyrus	Zephyr anglewing
Nymphalis antiopa	Mourning cloak
Nymphalis milberti	Milbert's tortoiseshell

Admirals, monarch, and painted ladies: medium to
large size; bright patterns

Danaus plexippus	Monarch
Vanessa cardui	Painted lady
Vanessa annabella	West Coast lady
Limenitis lorquini	Lorquin's admiral

Wood nymphs and arctics: dull yellow, brown, and
gray

Coenonympha tullia	Ochre ringlet
Cercyonis pegala	Pegala wood nymph
Cercyonis oetus	Oetus wood nymph
Oeneis nevadensis	Nevada arctic
Erebia epipsodea	Butler's alpine

Blues: small size; upper side blue (males) or brown (females); underside gray with black and sometimes orange spots

Glaucopsyche lygdamus	Silvery blue
Plebejus saepiolus	Greenish blue
Plebejus icarioides	Icarioides blue
Plebejus acmon	Acmon blue
Plebejus melissa	Melissa blue
Plebejus shasta	Shasta blue
Philotes battoides	Battoides blue
Everes amyntula	Tailed blue
Phaedrotes piasus	Arrowhead blue
Celastrina argiolus	Spring azure

Coppers: small size; mainly copper, tan, or blue with black spots

Lycaena mariposa	Mariposa copper
Lycaena editha	Edith's copper
Lycaena helloides	Purplish copper
Lycaena nivalis	Lilac-bordered copper
Lycaena rubidus	Ruddy copper
Lycaena cupreus	Lustrous copper
Lycaena heteronea	Blue copper

Hairstreaks: small size; often tails; often dark with patterned underside

Satyrium californica	California hairstreak
Satyrium fuliginosum	Sooty hairstreak
Satyrium behrii	Behr's hairstreak
Callophrys dumetorum	Green hairstreak
Callophrys spinetorum	Thicket hairstreak
Callophrys eryphon	Pine elfin
Callophrys nelsoni	Nelson's hairstreak
Habrodais grunus	Grunus hairstreak

Swallowtails: large size; tails

Papilio indra	Indra swallowtail
Papilio rutulus	Western tiger swallowtail
Papilio multicaudatus	Two-tailed swallowtail
Papilio zelicaon	Anise swallowtail
Papilio eurymedon	Mountain swallowtail

Skippers: dark; thick, hairy bodies

Erynnis propertius	Propertius' dusky wing skipper
Pyrgus ruralis	Checkered skipper
Hesperia juba	Juba skipper

Colias occidentalis   Western Sulphur

This male sulphur is holding his wings together vertically, which displays the underside. The forewing is clear yellow except for a black spot, whereas the hind wing is dusted with dark scales and has a pearl spot. The solid black band bordering the upper surface, which characterizes the male, is faintly visible through the wings. The western sulphur is often seen flying very rapidly across meadows east of the Cascades. The larvae feed on legumes. A different sulphur, the alfalfa butterfly — recognized by its row of black spots on the underside — is common near farms, especially east of the Cascades.

18

Pieris rapae   Cabbage White

The cabbage is a European butterfly introduced inadvertently to this continent in the nineteenth century. Lacking natural restraints in its new environment, it has steadily expanded its territory over most of North America, apparently to the disadvantage of our indigenous species of the same genus. **Pieris rapae** prospers around intensively developed urban regions where few other butterflies are seen. The appetite of its larvae for garden vegetables even has a slight economic impact. The life cycle is repeated two or three times each year, and the adults are in evidence from early spring until fall.

Pieris napi   Veined White

Rapae's gain seems to have been **napi**'s loss. As its unwelcome European relative has taken over the open regions across the continent, the veined white has literally retired mainly to the shaded seclusion of its woods, where it is one of the few butterflies to be found. The larvae of both species feed on the cabbage and mustard family. Yet, unsuccessful competition for available food hardly seems a convincing explanation by itself for **napi**'s retreat, in view of the tiny fraction of vegetation actually consumed. The veined white is slightly yellowish. The only markings are subdued stripes along the branching struts reinforcing the wings. These struts are called veins.

Pieris occidentalis   Western White

The female is pictured. In the male, the dark markings are much reduced. The western white is almost ubiquitous but is most prevalent in open fields and on mountains. It is often encountered flitting about the very summit of a hill or high mountain.

Anthocaris sara   Sara's Orange Tip

This is our only white butterfly with prominent orange patches. The female has a yellowish tinge. The underside of both sexes is marbled with green much like that illustrated for the marble wing. Sara's orange tip never moves very fast but seldom stops to rest. The adult is one of the earliest to emerge and may be seen on sunny days in late March. It is widely distributed in many habitats. Spindle-shaped eggs, initially orange but later fading, are attached by their tips to stems of wild mustard.

Euchloe ausonides   Marble Wing

A butterfly's compound eyes — one especially noticeable in this photo — are located near the base of the antennae or feelers. The multiple, separate facets of the eyes are better suited for perceiving motion than for image focusing. The marble wing is a spring butterfly, creamy or ivory with black markings above and marbled with green beneath. It prefers open country of the Columbia Basin, especially creek beds and hilltops. In the mountains, of course, it emerges later. The marble wing is not found west of the Cascades.

23

Parnassius clodius Clodius Parnassian

The apparent dark areas on the forewings of this
butterfly are actually transparent and caused by an unusual
local absence of the scales which normally make the
wings opaque. Two species of this genus may be found in
the Pacific Northwest: **clodius,** shown here feeding on
penstemon nectar, has solid black antennae; **phoebus** has
black and white, banded antennae. The clodius
parnassian is common in June and July along roads,
streams, and other clearings from sea level to the
Cascade Mountain crest, also occurring in the Blue
Mountains and the Wallowas. For a large butterfly, its flight
is flutteringly weak.

Speyeria callippe   Callippe Fritillary

Fritillaries are large brownish orange butterflies with black markings on the top side and silver or pearl spots on the underside of the hind wing (where species identification rests). It's easy to recognize a fritillary, but distinguishing one species from another is sometimes a different matter. There are some clues that will lead to the correct species identification in most cases. When confusion exists, it is certainly acceptable for one simply to enjoy nature's taste for variation and let others worry over details of its categorization.

Speyeria callippe Callippe Fritillary

The callippe fritillary is shown on these pages, displaying its
upper surface while resting on dogbane (opposite) and
its underside while feeding on mint. The greenish tone
and elongated silver spots on the underside of the hind wing
are characteristic features of most **callippe**s.

Speyeria zerene   Zerene Fritillary

Since butterflies ordinarily avoid danger by keeping on
the move, they are vulnerable during the ten- to
fifteen-minute period of mating. This pair of zerene fritillaries
has dropped down into the seclusion of grass and weeds.
Sperm is transferred from the abdomen of the male to the
oviduct of the female where it is stored. The eggs,
perhaps a hundred, will subsequently be fertilized as they
are extruded from the tip of her abdomen and deposited
on violets over a period of several days. **Zerene**'s
underside has large silver spots on a background color
ranging from light tan to brown.

Speyeria hydaspe   Hydaspe Fritillary

Fritillaries are very much attracted to thistles, dogbane,
and patches of mint blooming during July in the dry,
open woods dispersed through the mountains east of the
Cascade crest. The hydaspe fritillary is common along
roadsides and in other openings in the mountain forests. It
can generally be separated rather easily from other
fritillaries by the purplish maroon color of its underside and
by the pearl, not silver, spots.

29

Speyeria mormonia   Mountain Fritillary

The mountain fritillary is slightly smaller than other fritillaries. The black markings are delicate, creating a relatively pale appearance. The spots on the underside often are not silvered and are generally indistinct. This species is restricted to moist meadows at higher altitudes. Those pictured are at 7,000 feet near the shore of Fish Lake on Steens Mountain, Oregon. The mountain fritillary can also be seen flying in the meadows as you drive on U.S. Highway 26 through Oregon's Ochoco Mountains and at Chinook Pass near Mount Rainier National Park, Washington.

Speyeria leto   Leto Fritillary

The underside of the hind wing on this large male is
chocolate brown with a yellow marginal band. The spots
are sparse but well silvered. The upper side is a brighter
orange than that of most other fritillaries. The yellow
background color of the female is strikingly different. **Leto** is
found in the foothills in sunny fields near woods. It occurs in
scattered colonies throughout the Northwest. As with
many other fritillaries, its larvae eat the leaves of violets.
The larvae are seldom seen, apparently hiding during the
day and feeding only at night.

larva

Euphydryas colon   Snowberry Checkerspot

Medium-sized dark butterflies seen from the car in June
and July along dusty roads in the Cascades are likely to
be snowberry checkerspots. They are vigorous fliers and
before long have invariably battered themselves until they
appear dull and shabby. Closer inspection of this fresh
individual, however, reveals its striking yellow and brick
red spots. This full-grown prickly larva feeding on snowberry
leaves in May pupated three days later.

Boloria selene   Silver-bordered Fritillary

Boloria species are commonly called fritillaries, but they are not members of the genus **Speyeria. Boloria** look like undersized **Speyeria.** The silver-bordered fritillary has silver spots on the underside. It occurs broadly across Canada, but in this region, it is sharply limited to a few widely separated colonies occupying marshes where violets grow. Some of these colonies occupy only a few acres, apparently remnants left from a previous colder climate. Although the larvae can survive on ordinary wood violets, the adults are so rigorously adapted to the moist marsh habitat that they never stray elsewhere to deposit eggs.

Boloria epithore   Western Meadow Fritillary

The western meadow fritillary has a characteristic purple
tone to the underside of its hind wings. It is common in
the late spring in fields of western Washington and Oregon,
and in the summer at mid-altitudes in the Cascade and
Olympic mountains. The larvae feed on violets. **Boloria
titania** is a very similar butterfly found in August high in
the Washington Cascades and the Olympics, but not in
Oregon. **Titania** can be distinguished from **epithore** by the
prominent, sharply angled yellow markings on its underside.

Phyciodes campestris   Field Crescent

The field crescent inhabits meadows and forest clearings in the mountains from the Cascades through the Rockies as well as the Olympics. The adults are out in the summer. Crescents are small; the wingspan is about one and one-quarter inches. The underside has a cream and buff checkered pattern. On another day, a dragonfly was seen solemnly munching an unfortunate field crescent, the wings protruding from the dragon's mouth, bobbing limply up and down.

Phyciodes mylitta   Mylitta Crescent

The mylitta crescent, appearing brighter because of its finer black markings, occurs at lower elevations than the field crescent and is at least as common west as it is east of the Cascades. Undaunted by urban spread, it abounds around vacant lots and unattended scrubby fields, where the small, black, spiny larvae can be found on thistle. With multiple broods, the adults fly from March through October.

Polygonia zephyrus Zephyr Anglewing

The irregular edges of the anglewings give them a tattered appearance. Zephyr occurs principally in mountains but overlaps with satyr and resembles it in its habits. The upper surface is similar to satyr, but the underside of zephyr is gray rather than brown. The larvae feed on gooseberries and other plants. The adults are most common in the spring and late summer.

Polygonia satyrus Satyr Anglewing

The satyr is our most common anglewing, at least in populated places where it is likely to be observed. It occurs along roadsides and watercourses near woods where its larval food plant, nettle, grows. The aggressive male adults fly at other insects and apparently even make passes at birds that approach their perch. The underside of the wings is brown, patterned like a dead leaf.

38

Nymphalis antiopa   Mourning Cloak

The mourning cloak may be discovered almost anywhere at any time but is nowhere abundant. Adults hibernate and are sometimes seen flying about on sunny winter days. The larvae feed on willow and other trees, and an adult male will patrol back and forth over a stretch of stream bank or other sunny opening at the edge of the woods. This one is resting on a willow to which the butterfly repeatedly returned, each time choosing a different branch, usually not quite on the outside of the tree but recessed a little into the boughs, half in the sun, half in the shade.

Nymphalis milberti   Milbert's Tortoiseshell

Milbert's tortoiseshell occurs in varied habitats and may be very numerous in mountain meadows. It's certain to be noticed on the wildflowers by alpine hikers. Light green eggs are laid in masses on the underside of a nettle leaf, and the larvae remain in colonies until nearly full-grown. Look for the black larvae on nettle that has partially eaten, ragged leaves. The larvae can easily be raised to adulthood. The pupa is bronzed when new. Three weeks later the fully developed butterfly, ready to burst forth, can be seen enfolded within the transparent shell.

eggs

larvae

pupa

pupa

Danaus plexippus Monarch

In the Northwest, the monarch is a transient summer resident.
Virtually all of our other butterflies must cope with the full
cycle of seasons as offered by their local breeding
habitat, but the monarchs either migrate far to the south
in the fall or die. Adults reaching their destination in southern
California live through the winter often in huge colonies,
and in the following spring their progeny begin the long
return. Successive broods move northward, rearing their
young on milkweed, eventually reaching into Canada
before the cold autumn turns them back.

Vanessa annabella   West Coast Lady

The West Coast lady looks much like its more cosmopolitan
relative. It is a little smaller, and the distal forewing bar,
white on the painted lady, is pale orange on the West
Coast lady. Fresh adults are sometimes seen after frosts
as late as November.

Vanessa cardui   Painted Lady

Transporting pollen between blossoms is a fair trade for
the thistle's nectar. The painted lady has difficulty
surviving cold winters, and its temporary colonization in our
territory depends upon annual migration from more
southerly regions. Despite a worldwide distribution, the
painted lady usually occurs only sparingly in the
Northwest, but in occasional years massive migrations
occur. The larvae also feed on thistle. The upper side of the
adult resembles that of the West Coast lady.

Limenitis lorquini   Lorquin's Admiral

Its flight, usually along a path or some other clearing, is so distinctive that the admiral can be recognized by it — successive bursts of rapid flapping alternating with gliding, wings held out very horizontally. Lorquin's admiral is less interested in flowers than animal droppings, carrion, and decaying fruit. Three adults feeding on a snake crushed on the pavement returned repeatedly after passing cars temporarily interrupted their meal. The larvae have plainer tastes: willow, cottonwood, and poplar. This large, striking butterfly occurs over the entire Northwest.

Coenonympha tullia   Ochre Ringlet

The ochre ringlet is one of the most common Northwest
butterflies. This dainty little ringlet is almost plain ochre,
those east of the Cascade Range having a few small
eyespots. There is more than one brood each year, and
adults are seen from spring until autumn. They spend most of
their time flying near the ground in a lazy up-and-down
path, never far from the grasses upon which, as green
larvae, they fed.

Cercyonis pegala   Pegala Wood Nymph

In the morning when it is not yet hot in their shaded habitat, the wood nymphs like to warm themselves in the patches of sunlight falling between trees. The camouflage pattern of this mating pair blends subtly with the ponderosa pine bark. Larvae that hatch from the eggs will hibernate as infants and feed on grass next spring. Adults emerge in summer. These wood nymphs may also be found in sunny, open spaces. The upper surface of the wings is plain brown except for eyespots on the forewings, small in the male and large in the female.

Cercyonis oetus   Oetus Wood Nymph

The oetus wood nymph is slightly smaller than **pegala** (average wingspan, one and one-half inches), usually darker, and has a more uniform tone on the underside, relieved by fine, complicated zigzags and a conspicuous eyespot on the forewing. The upper surface is brown with eyespots. **Oetus** usually is found around open fields or in sagebrush country east of the Cascades from June through August. Neither species of wood nymph is likely to be seen in high mountains.

51

Oeneis nevadensis   Nevada Arctic

It's not easy to get close to the aloof arctic. The Nevada
is a swift flier and perches only tentatively on some vantage
point. When resting, its bright tawny upper surface is
hidden, and the gray and brown underside blends
effectively against the background of bark or branches
which it typically chooses. Unlike most other arctics which
live above timberline, this species prefers the open shade
of the forest. The Nevada arctic is found in the Cascade
Mountains. The life cycle lasts two years, and the adults
are found almost exclusively during even-numbered years.

Erebia epipsodea   Butler's Alpine

Species of this genus are generally alpine or arctic and in North America reside primarily in the Rocky Mountains and the Far North. Butler's alpine reaches westward into the North Cascades, Wallowas, and even the Ochocos, where it is seen in wet meadows usually below timberline. The larvae feed on grasses and hibernate through the severe winter when only half-grown. The dark brown adults are in flight in June and July. The males have less orange than is found on the illustrated female.

Glaucopsyche lygdamus   Silvery Blue

The blues are small, wingspan about one inch. The upper surface of the wings is usually bright blue, but females of several species are brownish blue or brown instead. Prismatic structure, not pigment, is responsible for the iridescent color; the blue disappears when the wings are wet. The silvery blue can be identified by its underside, which is illustrated in the cover photograph. It is a common butterfly in the early spring at low altitudes and in the summer in mountain meadows.

Plebejus saepiolus   Greenish Blue

The greenish blue has more numerous spots than the silvery blue and has a few modest orange crescents at the rear of the hind wing. The larvae feed on clover. This female (note brownish tint) resting on a clover blossom is not feeding but instead has her abdomen thrust forward as if preparing to deposit an egg. The upper side is blue, suffused with brown in the female. The greenish blue is found throughout this region in moist meadows, especially in the mountains.

Plebejus icarioides   Icarioides Blue

Blues are fond of drinking from mud, and none more so than **icarioides.** This one has found a patch of broken earth moistened by a spring. Watch for wet spots along the trail. Butterflies become preoccupied while drinking, and their undersides can usually be examined closely enough to identify the different species of blues. **Icarioides** has black spots rimmed by white, the black more prominent on the forewing, the white predominating on the hind wing. Its range covers the entire Northwest.

Plebejus acmon   Acmon Blue

The underside of the acmon blue is well displayed by this
male clinging to a delicate seed pod. At this close
range, it can be seen that each orange spot is tipped
by a few greenish, metallic scales, an almost extravagantly
beautiful detail. (How many others pass by us unnoticed!)
On the upper surface the male is purplish blue, the
female brown with blue lights. The orange spots are
repeated on the upper surface where they form a confluent
band. **Acmon** is found east of the Cascades on the dry
foothills which come down to the prairie. The adults are
on wild buckwheat flowers from May through September.

Plebejus melissa   Melissa Blue

The Melissa blue has orange spots with metallic crescents on
its underside similar to those of **acmon** but occurring on the
forewing as well as the hind wing. In the female the
orange repeats on the upper surface, whereas the
male is solid bright blue above. This female is getting her
day started by warming up in the morning sun. It is
midsummer, but the foliage is fresh in the Ochoco
Mountains. **Melissa** is scattered rather sparingly east of
the Cascades — through the dry open mountain forests and
the basin areas. As with many other blues, the larvae feed
on legumes.

Plebejus shasta Shasta Blue

The shasta blue has metallic marks but no more than a trace of orange coloring. It is a little smaller than most other blues. The shasta blue is limited in Oregon to a few mountains and has yet to be reported in Washington. It seems to thrive on adversity. We photographed this one resting on the alpine vegetation at 9,000 feet on Steens Mountain, where the colony is confined to within 100 yards of the ridge at the very summit. To avoid being swept away by the unremitting wind, these tiny blues were restricting their flight to only a few inches above the ground.

Philotes battoides   Battoides Blue

The battoides blue is very similar to **acmon,** except that the orange usually is a little reduced and the dark spots of the underside are heavier. It resides predominantly in mountains. In the Okanogan Highlands several battoides blues were congregated at a coyote dropping, feeding through their long, slender tongues. Occasionally one would fly up, only to return shortly. They exhibited no interest whatever in the far more plentiful droppings from herbivorous horses strewn along the same trail.

Everes amyntula   Tailed Blue

A wild strawberry blossom makes a perfect pedestal for the tailed blue, the only blue with tails in this area. The underside is silvery white with a single minute orange and green spot on the hind wing. The upper side is blue. A moist sunny glen surrounded by trees is the usual habitat.

Phaedrotes piasus   Arrowhead Blue

The underside of the arrowhead blue is dark, warm gray with prominent and characteristic black and white markings, the latter apparently suggesting to someone a row of arrowheads pointing towards the base of the hind wing. The upper side is deep blue with a black-and-white-banded fringe. Not common, this species occurs in scattered colonies in canyons and open mountain terrain ranging from the Cascades through the Rockies. In flight, it can tentatively be distinguished from other blues by its slightly larger size and darker color.

Celastrina argiolus *Spring Azure*

The spring azure, among the earliest adult butterflies to emerge, occurs throughout the United States. It is the most common blue in the urban areas of western Oregon and Washington. Gregarious at its water holes, crowds of this little butterfly may be seen in April or May at wet spots along the Eagle Creek trail in the Columbia Gorge. The underside is pale with numerous, rather indistinct spots. The upper side is blue, bright in the male and dark in the female. Dogwood is one of its many food plants.

Lycaena mariposa   Mariposa Copper

Coppers are small, wingspan one to one and one-half inches. The upper sides of most species range from brown to orange in the male and from yellow to orange with dark brown markings in the female. The underside provides the key to identification. This is a female mariposa copper, alighting first with her wings held out flat and then with them vertical. On its underside the forewing is predominantly yellow and the hind wing finely stippled gray. The mariposa copper is common where the forest and tundra meet in the Pasayten Wilderness in northern Washington. A late summer mountain butterfly, this copper is still on the wing, flitting among the wildflowers along the high trails, even into October when the first snows begin to fall.

Lycaena editha Edith's Copper

The markings of Edith's copper are conservative but elegant: brown spots carefully outlined in white and a restrained orange stripe against a tan background. The upper side is dull brown, solid in the male and interrupted by yellow in the female. The larvae feed on **Potentilla.** Edith's copper, not common, is most likely to be encountered in mountains east of the Cascades.

Lycaena helloides Purplish Copper

The purplish copper's name refers to the iridescent purple
sheen of the brown upper surface of the male. The
picture shows the underside with the prominent orange
zigzag line near the trailing edge of the beige hind wing. The
marshy surroundings are typical for this species. The
purplish copper has more than one brood during a
season, and adults may be found from early spring into
autumn. It occurs mainly at low altitudes.

Lycaena nivalis Lilac-bordered Copper

When a butterfly sits in the open on a flat surface with wings held together vertically, it tends to line up with the sun so that it will not cast a large shadow which might give away its presence. This poses a problem for photography. We waited until this one turned enough for the sun to catch her beautiful yellow and lilac hind wing, which characterizes the lilac-bordered copper.

Lycaena rubidus Ruddy Copper

The male ruddy copper can be recognized at a glance. No other copper has the same fiercely bright, solid red color. Brown markings are superimposed on this background in the upper side of the female. The underside is pale cream, sometimes with small dark spots. You will see the ruddy copper in midsummer in arid eastern Washington and Oregon, a red jewel on goldenrod or a metallic glint across rabbit brush in the flat open prairie.

Lycaena heteronea   Blue Copper

A copper that is blue enough to be a blue. The underside is pale gray, usually with black spots. The upper side of the male is bright blue, that of the female is more like other coppers. The blue copper is a mountain meadow resident from the Cascades to the Rockies. It likes flowers. This one feeding on false buckwheat has his wings folded back, but males often alight with horizontal wings, displaying their beautiful blue upper surface.

Lycaena cupreus   Lustrous Copper

The upper surface of the lustrous copper is brilliant reddish copper with black spots and solid black border. On the underside the hind wing is gray and the forewing, reddish copper. This bright butterfly occurs in isolated alpine colonies throughout the West. It prefers inaccessible niches and has been found in only a few places in the Pacific Northwest. A mountaineer would be a likely person to discover a new colony on some inhospitable-looking windswept crag.

Satyrium californica   California Hairstreak

Hairstreaks are small, fast-flying butterflies of diverse appearance and habits. Many are brightly colored, especially on the underside, and some have delicate tails on the hind wings. The California hairstreak has a row of orange spots and one blue spot at the base of the tail. The upper side is brown with a dull orange spot on the hind wing. Ceanothus is the larval food. The adults are found in July in the foothills and open country from the Cascade Mountains eastward.

72

Satyrium fuliginosum   Sooty Hairstreak

The sooty hairstreak's name describes its dull, grayish brown color. The upper side is wholly without markings, and those on the underside are hardly striking. There are no tails. This inconspicuous butterfly may be mistaken for a worn blue, and in fact the larvae feed on lupine, a legume. The sooty hairstreak, a mountain species, is widespread in eastern Oregon and Washington at higher elevations and may be found in large numbers in midsummer on the alpine flowers above the Cloud Cap area of the northern slope on Mount Hood.

74

Satyrium behrii   Behr's Hairstreak

The dusty sage plain, stretched out and baking under the
July sun, may not look very promising for butterflies.
However, close inspection of this terrain is very likely to
disclose the handsome Behr's hairstreak. The upper
side is tawny near the base of the wings with a broad brown
band at the outer edge. This hairstreak is common east of
the Cascades into the Rockies. The larvae feed on
antelope brush.

Callophrys dumetorum   Green Hairstreak

You will encounter the green hairstreak in open, wooded
areas of the lower mountain slopes. The larvae feed on
legumes during the summer, and the adults emerge in
the early spring. The bright green underside of the wings
readily identifies this species once it is spotted, but also
effectively conceals the butterfly as it rests on the fresh
spring foliage. The upper surface is brown, light in
females and darker in males. Its flight is rapid and
erratic but never far.

Callophrys spinetorum   Thicket Hairstreak

Butterflies usually do not sit perfectly still. Hairstreaks can often be seen waving their antennae up and down or sliding their hind wings back and forth across each other in a slow, grinding rhythm. The underside of the thicket hairstreak shown here needs no further description, but the upper side is a surprising, shiny steel blue. This hairstreak occurs from the Cascades to the Rockies but, unfortunately, only sparingly. The thicket hairstreak larva is well camouflaged against its food plant — dwarf mistletoe, a parasite growing on conifers, in this case on hemlock branches.

77

Callophrys eryphon Pine Elfin

Distributed throughout the Northwest, the pine elfin is our most common hairstreak. This adult is perched on its larval food plant exposing its underside. As in many hairstreak species, the males have a small, dark patch, the "scent pad," on the upper surface near the leading edge of the forewing. These specialized scales produce substances involved in courtship.

Callophrys nelsoni   Nelson's Hairstreak

The light blue band and subtle brown and violet hues of
the underside of Nelson's hairstreak are well illustrated. The
fine tails can also be seen. The top surface is plain light
brown. Nelson's hairstreak flies with the pine and green
hairstreaks, or a little later. It is common on the eastern
slope of the Oregon Cascades and in Washington's wet
coniferous forests. On Memorial Day you can usually find
nelsoni on flowers along the Metolius River in Oregon and
at Lake Cushman in Washington. The larvae feed on
juniper or cedar.

Habrodais grunus   Grunus Hairstreak

The grunus hairstreak is distinctively yellow with only faint
marks. Its food plant in California is live oak, but to the
north **grunus** has thoroughly adapted its life cycle to
chinquapin. Adults feed on the short spikes of yellow flowers
in August, and the larvae hatch from overwintered eggs
late in the next spring when new, tender leaves have just
started. This butterfly lives within the range of its food
plant through the Oregon Cascades. It has not been
reported north of the Columbia River, but a careful search
might well uncover it there in Skamania County where
chinquapin can be found.

Papilio indra Indra Swallowtail

Indra is mostly black and has only very short tails. It is found in the dry, eastern portions of this region where its larval food plant, desert parsley, grows. Adults emerge in the spring. This butterfly was photographed in May on the open hills near Satus Pass, Washington, where **indra** occurs in rather large numbers.

Papilio rutulus   Western Tiger Swallowtail

The swallowtail in your yard probably is the western tiger.
It's usually seen at a frustrating distance, soaring high
among branches of a tree, pausing without actually
stopping, then away and out of sight, only to reappear ·
later from an unexpected direction. This male is
replenishing himself from a mock orange blossom
along a lane through the woods. Eggs are laid on willow,
aspen, and cottonwood. The green larvae with prominent
false eyespots are frequently discovered in August.

Papilio multicaudatus Two-Tailed Swallowtail

The two-tailed swallowtail is best identified by its pair of
double tails. It is also our largest swallowtail and is more
predominately yellow than the western tiger. Restricted to
the arid country east of the Cascades, it sails tirelessly up
and down canyons within reach of its food plant,
chokecherry. This butterfly is never plentiful. The symmetrical
nicks in the outer margins of both forewings were probably
made by the beak of a bird when the butterfly's wings
clapped together in an evasive flight maneuver.

Papilio zelicaon   Anise Swallowtail

The anise swallowtail manages to occupy essentially all
habitats of the Pacific Northwest and is the only swallowtail
reaching into truly alpine regions. This pair, in the Elkhorn
Mountains of eastern Oregon, is drinking from moist
earth in the July afternoon sun. Butterflies often associate in
tight clusters while drinking. This habit can probably be
traced to local attractive mineral deposits in the soil
rather than to a social motive. The larva has eaten the
desert parsley plant essentially to the ground. Any survival
advantage from its beautiful but conspicuous
appearance is difficult to understand. The pupa is firmly
attached by its tip to the stem and suspended by a
strong silk sling.

larva

pupa

87

Papilio eurymedon   Mountain Swallowtail

Serviceberry and wildflowers grow right along the bank of
the Metolius River under the tall ponderosa. The morning
air is still. Later it becomes hot and smells of pine resin.
We watched this male mountain swallowtail feed on wild
columbine. This is a typical habitat for the mountain
swallowtail, which ranges throughout the Pacific
Northwest and can be identified by its pale yellow or
almost white color. The larvae feed on ceanothus and alder.

Erynnis propertius   *Propertius' Dusky Wing Skipper*

Skippers are small-to-medium-sized butterflies which in some ways resemble moths. They have thick hairy bodies, fuzzy wings, and antennae that end in a compromise between a knob and a point. The dusky wing is found in the canyons and foothills on both sides of the Cascades where its food plant, oak, grows. The adults emerge in the early spring. Their somber appearance matches the persisting winter background of browns and grays.

Pyrgus ruralis   Checkered Skipper

This black and white skipper is widely distributed, but usually only isolated individuals are seen. Look for it in open meadows and fields in the spring and summer.

Hesperia juba Juba Skipper

Like most other skippers, **juba** has an extremely rapid, darting flight which is difficult to follow. The strength of its wing muscles is very apparent when one of these skippers is held lightly between your fingers. **Juba** occurs all over the Northwest, but prefers moderately arid territory, where it is often numerous. The larvae feed on grass, and the adults are in flight from the spring through the fall.

Index